gratitude
prayers

Amazing Graces
Animal Blessings
Baby Blessings
Back to Joy
Bedside Prayers
Bless the Beasts
Bless the Day
Christmas Blessings
Comfort Prayers
Dog Blessings
Family Celebrations
Forever in Love
Garden Blessings
Get Well Wishes
Graces
Heal Your Soul, Heal the World
The Home Design Handbook
House Blessings
Looking for God in All the Right Places
Miracles of Motherhood
Mothers and Daughters
Pocket Prayers
Say a Little Prayer: A Journal
Serenity Prayers
Soar! Follow Your Dreams
Teen Sunshine Reflections
To Have and To Hold
Toasts
Wedding Blessings
Wishing You Well

gratitude prayers

Prayers, Poems, and Prose for Everyday Thankfulness

June Cotner

Andrews McMeel Publishing®

Kansas City · Sydney · London

Andrews McMeel Publishing, LLC
an Andrews McMeel Universal company
1130 Walnut Street, Kansas City, Missouri 64106

www.andrewsmcmeel.com

15 16 17 18 19 SDB 10 9 8 7 6 5

ISBN: 978-1-4494-2176-2

Library of Congress Control Number: 2012943307

Book design by Holly Ogden

ATTENTION: SCHOOLS AND BUSINESSES
Andrews McMeel books are available at quantity discounts with
bulk purchase for educational, business, or sales promotional use.
For information, please e-mail the Andrews McMeel Publishing
Special Sales Department: specialsales@amuniversal.com.

No halos, no wings.
Dedicated to all those everywhere
who spread kindness
every day.

CONTENTS

∽ *three* ∽

THE NATURAL WORLD 27

∽ *four* ∽

FRIENDS & FAMILY 43

✎ *five* ✎
JOY & WONDER 59

✒ eight ✒

REFLECTIONS 97

thanks

I am thankful for the contributors who sent me eloquent gems for this book. I'm also grateful to everyone who submitted to this book. Your words inspire me!

This is now the sixth book I've created for Andrews McMeel Publishing. Through the creation of all of these books, my editor has been Patty Rice. Patty, do you remember about eight years ago at BookExpo America you told me that you wanted to do a book on "joy?" Well, the kernel of your idea grew into *Gratitude Prayers*!

Denise Marcil and Anne Marie O'Farrell at Marcil-O'Farrell Literary: I love our creative brainstorming sessions and I greatly appreciate all of the good ideas you both bring to my work.

I am forever grateful to my husband, Jim, and my many relatives and friends who encourage and inspire me every day.

And to God, I live in thankfulness for all of the blessings in my life.

letter to readers

Gratitude Prayers was a treasure to create! I noticed I was smiling throughout *all* the stages of this book, from the first idea to the final manuscript. As I read the hundreds of submissions for *Gratitude Prayers*, the thoughts and reflections offered by contributors gave me an even deeper appreciation for the gift of life.

Is there a link between gratitude and prayer? I think there's a big one. The more we focus on the joy in our lives, the more satisfied we feel. Studies by Robert A. Emmons, the world's leading scientific expert on gratitude, have shown that feelings of gratitude led to more positive emotional states and inspired people to be more helpful to others. He found that people who regularly practice grateful thinking can increase their level of happiness by as much as 25 percent. In his book *Thanks! How the New Science of Gratitude Can Make You Happier*, he encourages people to learn prayers of gratitude.

Praying guides us through both good times and bad. During periods when it's hard to keep a positive attitude, you can turn to the chapter Faith & Courage for ideas on how to get through difficult circumstances. If your perspective becomes bleak, prayer can turn you around. The writers in *Gratitude Prayers* share how to seek out tiny moments of joy, which will point the way toward finding the good in every situation.

With *Gratitude Prayers,* you will become a "noticer" of people and surroundings that delight you. The selections in this book will encourage you to pay attention to things that make you laugh, the places that nourish you, the loved ones who inspire and guide you, and caring strangers who bring blessings to your days.

I encourage you to leave *Gratitude Prayers* in a place where you will see it throughout the day. Make it *your* book; feel free to make notes in the margins where you can date and note how a particular prayer or poem helped you. You can use a selection as a springboard to reflect on what was good that day.

Using *Gratitude Prayers* will nudge you toward a deeper gratefulness for life. Over time, finding gratitude will become a habit and a powerful force for influencing those around you. Don't we all love to be around a person who is genuinely grateful?

As you go through your day, may the selections in *Gratitude Prayers* help you recognize the sacred in the ordinary—the moments that bring you everyday thankfulness. It is my hope that this collection will serve as a reminder to continually seek an attitude of gratitude in every situation.

one

SIMPLE PLEASURES

All that we behold is full of blessings.

ᕲ WILLIAM WORDSWORTH (1770–1850)

MIRACLES
(Excerpt)

Why, who makes much of a miracle?
As to me I know of nothing else but miracles,
Whether I walk the streets of Manhattan . . .
Or look at strangers opposite me riding in the car,
Or watch honey-bees busy around the hive
of a summer forenoon,
Or animals feeding in the fields,
Or birds . . .
Or the wonderfulness of the sundown, or of stars
shining so quiet and bright,
Or the exquisite delicate thin curve of the new
moon in spring . . .

To me every hour of the light and dark is a miracle,
Every cubic inch of space is a miracle,
Every square yard of the surface of the earth is
   spread with the same . . .
What stranger miracles are there?

⌐ WALT WHITMAN (1819–1892)

HOLY TOMATOES

I pluck tomatoes from the vines,
feel them sun-warmed and firm in my hands.
Such gifts arriving in our daily dirt.

Light pours through the window
as I rinse them in the sink.
Water droplets shimmer,
poised on skins red as love.

I am held here, like the dust motes
floating in a beam of light,
caught in that sunstream.

How the world offers itself up.
Sunlight spills through the window
and the tomatoes glow, opulent spheres
each one round, full, complete.

↪ GINNY LOWE CONNORS

SURPRISED

Like a baby
seeing her shadow
for the first time,
we notice joy.

Was it there all the time?
Did we only need
stand in the light
to discover it?

↜ MARYANNE HANNAN

Morning

There is so much life still undone
so much still in bloom.

— DENISE LEVERTOV

Each morning I wake
with excitement

overwhelmed by the leaves
turning outside the window,

the scent of fall,
the slant of morning light,

the books on my nightstand
filled with promise

the books on the coffee table
in the living room where you sit

already awake
in the unfolding of day

reading or writing, coffee in hand,
looking up and smiling, as you do.

～ MICHAEL S. GLASER

Simple Pleasures

I took a hot bath last night.
As the tub filled, I marveled at the process.
I was grateful.
I did not have to fetch the water,
Nor build a fire to warm it.
I did not have to carry it,
Heavy, one bucket at a time,
Taking care not to slosh it,
Up the flights of stairs to the second-floor tub.
I simply turned a handle.
There it poured,
Water, flowing uphill,
Hot, clean, refreshing, abundant.
Thank you, God, for simple pleasures
That really aren't that simple, after all.

⌐ SUSANNE WIGGINS BUNCH

GENTLE THINGS

Thank You for
gentle
things—the
glow of
morning light,
the swaying
of a towering
tree, the
humming of a
tiny bee,
the soft approach
of night.

∽ THOMAS L. REID

SUNDAY AFTERNOON AT MUNSINGER GARDENS

We sit on a blanket on the grass and listen to jazz
as bits of fluff fall from the cottonwood trees,
a hint of snow on this sunny summer day.

Six ducklings follow their mother out of the
   underbrush
and topple into the Mississippi River. The feathers
of the mallards nearby, all flamboyant greens

and purples; sunlight glittering on the deep blue
of the water. The mother duck squawks and flaps
her wings until the other ducks have scattered.

Then she swims serenely around the ducklings,
ignoring the rustle of wings around her
as if nothing at all has happened.

I feed the baby from a cup of vanilla
ice cream and he gives me a kiss
that's both sweet and pleasantly sticky.

The people behind us are talking
over the music, the grass is damp under our blanket.
I feel so happy that it's almost painful.

Sunday afternoon, the river shining
silver and blue in the sun, ducklings
tracing lazy circles in the water,

shade trees on either side, and in
the distance, almost too far away to see,
the bridge leading back toward home.

↬ LEAH BROWNING

HAPPINESS

She loves West Tenth Street on an
ordinary summer morning.

⁋ MICHAEL CUNNINGHAM, *THE HOURS*

And I love *this* ordinary summer afternoon,
sitting under my cherry tree full of overripe fruit,
too much for us to pick, an abbondanza of a tree,
I love this dark gray catbird singing its awkward
song, and the charcoal clouds promising rain
they don't deliver. I love the poem I've been trying
to write for months, but can't; I love the way
it's going nowhere at all. I love the dried grass
that crackles when you walk on it,
leached of color, its own kind of fire.
Way off in the hedgerow, the musical olio
of dozens of birds, each singing its own song,

each beating its own measure. This is all there is:
the red cherries, the green leaves, sky like a pale
silk dress, and the rise and fall of the sweet
breeze. Sometimes, just what you have
manages to be enough.

∽ BARBARA CROOKER

Gifts

What gives a gift its value
   is sentiment and thought.
It's not determined by the cost
   for love cannot be bought.

Homemade gifts can warm the heart
   and always bring a smile
For love's the main ingredient
   that makes a gift worthwhile.

Store-bought gifts can be exchanged,
   returned or thrown away,
But something made by loving hands
   grows fonder day by day.

∾ CLAY HARRISON

two

EVERYDAY LIFE

*Let us savor the most fleeting delights
of our most beautiful days!*

∽ ALPHONSE DE LAMARTINE (1790–1869)

NO NEED TO WORRY

Good morning,
This is God!
I will be handling all of your problems today.
I will not need your help—
so have a great day.

∽ AUTHOR UNKNOWN

A Bit of Joy

Days run into nights, nights into days;
we adapt, we adjust,
to ever-changing challenges.

A stranger once said to me,
"I pray you may find a moment of joy
in each day." That loving bit of wisdom
has inspired me to search for that gleam
of unexpected joy which lifts me up again.

Faith sustains . . .
Family stays close . . .
Friends uphold . . .
Music soothes . . .
Books can bring respite . . .
For all that, I am grateful.
Each may bring that moment of joy in what may be
an otherwise intense day.

⌇ BETTY ANN LEAVITT

THE WASH PRAYER

On the best days I offer
this invisible work, this work
so easily undone.
So when the memory of sleep
is smoothed from beds,
when breakfast bowls return
to their cupboard I begin
the litany of laundry
sadly astonished to see again
the hill of clothes slumped
in the wicker basket,
all their pride gone, their lives
inhabiting other garments.
And if it's a good day I lovingly
sort dark socks and wadded trousers
from the baby's white T-shirts
and his sister's pastels.

Into the vessel, faithful as a truck,
they go, to churn and swirl
in their mysterious froth
making shapes I cannot see.
And after the dryer revives
each wet skin I sit
and fold these clothes into
safety, health, laughter, home.

～ LISA ZIMMERMAN

EARLY MORNING
GRATITUDE CHECK

Tea kettle on the stove. Check.
Purring cat on the couch. Check.
Furnace rumbling in the basement. Check.
Family sleeping upstairs. Check.
Day on the horizon. Check.
Gratitude within. Check and check.

∽ BARBARA YOUNGER

LET THE DAY BREAK

Let the rooster crow
like Nature's alarm clock
that rouses resting Earth.

Let the day break
with a bright sun that peeps
through blackness of Night's sky.

As the Sun climbs
with welcome warmth,
let the day break

for the owl returning to roost,
for farmers preparing
to work in their fields and meadows.

Let the day break
with joy and gratitude
for new beginnings and fresh starts.

᙭ SANDRA H. BOUNDS

THIS ORDINARY WORLD

To hear an oriole sing
May be a common thing
—Or only a divine.

⌐ EMILY DICKINSON

At the bus stop waiting for our children
the women talk. I listen
to their voices babbling
letting the steady flow
of conversation wash over me and
join with the sound of the oriole
whistling in a nearby tree.
A breeze sighs through tree branches
stirring a symphony of leaf-song
rustling and caressing the air.

The bus soon appears
sounding a cha-cha-cha
on the black asphalt street.

All seems to come to a halt
as the bus screeches to a stop.

Then bus doors open. Laughter and chatter
greet waiting parents
as children noisily descend
bus stairs.

Music fills the air—
songs of everyday life
in this ordinary world.

෴ SHERRI WAAS SHUNFENTHAL

THIS BODY

Happy, I listen to the tinny sounds
of the great music I still hear.

Dazzling clear pure upper tones
have disappeared but I am alive,

silvery and achy—like Beethoven
I listen with my imagination not my senses

to the cascading notes that play
on the cosmos, I listen with my heart

and dance to the bliss I would never have known
without this human body.

⮫ JANINE CANAN

Both Ways

I like to get home first.
Put away my stuff.
Freshen up.
Greet my love with a hug and a kiss.

And

I like to get home last.
See the light on.
Smell dinner.
Be given a hug and a kiss when I walk in the door.

I like to get home.

∽ CINDY BREEDLOVE

MORNING LIGHT

Each day the soul decides whether
or not to enter yet one more time
into this carousel, blinks open
the body's eyes to nearly
morning light, lifts the head
in glory to God's vast sky,
climbs the legs out of bed
to keep moving on this
journey to understanding
the mystery and beauty
of being alive.

❧ BARBARA SCHMITZ

three

THE NATURAL WORLD

Magical things happen every day, if we allow it.
Think of daylight, of the stars at night, a flower.
A dandelion is a miracle.

~ PAMELA TRAVERS (1899–1996)

THE THIRD BEATITUDE

Blessed was I today for I did inherit the earth
and the earth was constant and miraculous.
The winter wind chatted with the wind chimes
and was my morning wake-up call.
The hills wrapped themselves in resplendent
    ermine
and I walked among them with reflected elegance.
The air was laundered and crisply starched
and crinkled and crackled in my nose and lungs.
A sparrow danced about the hawthorn in a lively
    fandango
and I clapped my hands and shouted olé, olé!
Blessed was I today for I did inherit the earth
and the earth was constant and miraculous.

↝ SUSAN J. ERICKSON

APRIL, BY THE LITTLE JORDAN

So I'm sitting here by the laughing stream,
a buttery bunch of marsh marigolds nearby,
and when the wind blows through the phlox,
it's like the doors to a dozen bakeries, opening.
The afternoon drowses, round as a lemon.
Far off, cardinals converse in code: *chip chip chip*.
The pale green leaves of the black walnut tree
tat their lace overhead, and there, at my feet,
a small bit of eggshell, chip off the fallen sky.
The things that have been pressing me in,
weighing me down, seem far away as Canada.
I drift off, satiated, in the sugar-dusted air.

～ BARBARA CROOKER

INSTRUCTIONS

Leave your cell phone, your watch
and your thoughts
on the kitchen table.

Walk slowly. Leave the trail
to follow a scent
or to follow a bird's refrain.

Listen for the stirrings
in the underbrush.

Notice what grows at your feet,
the puzzle-pieces of the sky
and what the light reveals.

Cast out your gaze like a net
and take everything in

every intricate detail,
each small astonishment.

～ DEBORAH GORDON COOPER

No Other Joy

I want no other joy, when summer
comes back, than last year's joy.
Under sleeping muscats I shall sit.
In the heart of woods singing with fresh water,
I shall hear and feel and see
all that the forest hears, feels and sees.

I want no other joy, when autumn
comes back, than that of the yellow leaves
sweeping slopes amidst thunder,
than hushed new wine in barrels,
and heavy skies, and cow bells clanging,
and beggars asking for alms.

I want no other joy, when winter
comes back, than that of the iron sky,
than smoking, grinding cranes,
embers singing like the sea,
and a lamp by green tiles
at the shop where the bread is bitter.

I want no other joy, when spring
comes back, than that of the sharp wind,
than leafless peach trees in bloom,
and muddy paths going green,
and violets, and the songbird
gushing like a stream in the storm.

～ FRANCIS JAMMES (1868–1938)
translated by janine canan

May Day, Betpouey,
the Pyrenees

Last night a late spring snow,
and today, sun and this hike
to the Shrine of St. Justin.

The mountain guides streamlets
of melting snow in a dance
that rushes past the blossoming spring flowers

so that everything seems fragile and fleeting
and flowing through the canyons
to the rivers and ocean below.

I like to believe that all things connect
like this, that each life and spirit, each
flower and stream connects, connects,

and that, if we are kind enough,
one to the other, we might know that,
hear it in the river's song, in the mountain breeze,

see it in the snow, in the colors of clouds
praising the sun as it rises
praising the sun as it sets.

∽ MICHAEL S. GLASER

ON GUARDIAN ANGELS

Perhaps my angels have all along been birds.
How often am I out of their sight?
Even when I'm indoors, they come
to the window, seek me, keep watch.

So what if I can't understand their speech?
As long as the dawn hears the rooster and the waves
take their cue from the gulls, I too can have
their music without demanding sense of it.

In the main, my angels are small, brown sparrows,
who fly like tiny grapeshot and fastidiously watch,
but call little attention to themselves. They even seem
indifferent; but isn't that a perfect disguise?

～ RICHARD BEBAN

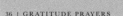

THE WILDING

Gardens of blossom in splendor,
Colors arranged as sown,
But none with beauty so rare
As the flower that stands alone.

Columbine and Indian pipe,
Lady's slipper of pink and gold;
Untamed treasures of nature
Are a glory to behold.

Fragile pixie of the wood,
No bouquet meant to be;
Bewitching is your charm
As long as you are free.

You bloom and die in solitude
Beyond the touch of care.
Your shining was not wasted–
God surely put you there.

∽ C. DAVID HAY

On Reading Genesis

. . . the spirit of God moving over the water

∽ GENESIS 1:2

I look at the ocean, the sky above.
Watch charcoal clouds cast shadows
on distant swells. Think of God.

Not a hovering God. No details,
yet I feel God's Holy presence
in the air we breathe.

I have no need to see God's image.
No need to see a benevolent persona—
the knowing is all that matters.

∽ DOROTHY WINSLOW WRIGHT

WITH ONE VOICE, RISING

Wisps of fog drift across
the waters. The Spirit of
God moves across the
waters, lifting our spirits,
moving us to praise. A
bird responds. A rooster
crows. Even at night in
the evening light beside
our pond, a lively throng
of frogs repeats the glad
chorus with one accord:
"Thank You. Thank You.
Thank. Thank. Thank."

~ MARY HARWELL SAYLER

MAGIC

We were talking about magic
as we drove along a crowded
Sunday highway

when the whir of wings
made me turn
and a flock of geese

flew over our car
so low I could see
their feet tucked under them.

For a moment the rustle
of their presence over our heads
obscured everything

and as they disappeared
you said,
"I see what you mean."

🙠 SUDIE NOSTRAND

BLESSINGS OF THE RAIN

I listen to the raindrops
Whispering through my open window,
Breathing their freshness into my soul.

Raindrops softly spreading
Over the lifted faces of flowers,
Urging my roots to grow once again.

I watch the blessings
Of the virgin rain
Unfold my thankful heart.

৵ TIRZI THERESE HEIDINGSFELD

four

FRIENDS & FAMILY

Let us be grateful to people who make us happy;
they are the charming gardeners
who make our souls blossom.

∽ MARCEL PROUST (1871–1922)

CELEBRATION

I want to celebrate you.
I am truly blessed to be a part of your world.
I learn from you, I admire you, I love you.
You are my own personal star that follows me
around and shines down on me.
You light my life with magic and wonder.
Such a gift of love.
You are a part of my soul.
You own a piece of my heart.
Your loving spirit provides a constant parade
of emotions that warm my heart.
I feel complete knowing you are near.
I feel empty without you.
I want to celebrate you,
yesterday, today, and tomorrow.

～ LORI EBERHARDY

OPEN HEARTS

They teach.
They guide.
They counsel.
They console.
They befriend.
They minister.
They lead.
They inspire.

Again and again
Each reprises
Just one lesson:
That we are valued,
That we are capable.

That is all.
That is everything.

⁓ DIANNE M. DEL GIORNO

WITH THE CHILDREN

The children
scream through the house,
bare feet padding on hardwood.

Dress up.
Darth Vader chasing
Disney Princess.
Lightsaber versus wand.

Sunday morning cinnamon rolls,
autumn crisp.

I've forgotten so much.
Please,
please let me keep more
than a photograph.
When age finally takes
the folds of my mind and collapses them,
when all goes gray, and confused,

Let me remember love.

〜 MICHAEL D. HEILMAN

BETWEEN YOU AND ME

You are here inside my laughter.
Thoughts of you are on my mind and
wrapped around my heart.
You empower me to love with all I have,
and to enjoy all that is good.
As I embrace each day with the promise of you,
I can't imagine a day that is not filled
with your smiles.
My life has been kissed by many blessings,
and because of you each day is a gift
filled with grace, mercy and love.
I cherish the moments that bring us together,
and it is inside this space I realize I am home.

✍ LORI EBERHARDY

THE POWER OF GRACE

How much I loved you!
Your smile, your embrace, your words
were stitches in the garment I donned each day.
Without them, I would have been naked,
my life bare.

Why did I think you were so mortal
I could love you only with my senses,
touching, hearing, seeing?
Now heart murmurings, warm feelings,
    cherished memories
tell me you are with me always.

And through your leaving, I learned about grace,
an unexpected gift which picked me up,
moved me forward, helped me recover.
And so now, I am left with two gifts:
That inexplicable grace. And you.

∽ DeMar Regier

FRIENDSHIP

Oh, the comfort—the inexpressible comfort of
feeling safe with a person,
Having neither to weigh thoughts,
Nor measure words—but pouring them
All right out—just as they are—
Chaff and grain together—
Certain that a faithful hand will
Take and sift them—
Keep what is worth keeping—
And with the breath of kindness
Blow the rest away.

∾ DINAH MARIA MULOCK CRAIK (1826–1887)

WALKING WITH DOG

I include as one of my best friends
The furry lover at the end of this leash
Who accepts me and my actions
With no strings attached

His eyes always show just what
He thinks is going on in my heart
He feels the vibrations of my anxiety
Travel the length of his leash

His gait tells me to slow down
To absorb all the looks and smells
Of the beauty that may pass us by
So I absorb all I can as he takes me for a walk

↬ GARY E. McCORMICK

An Angel in Disguise

A little angel was laid in my arms one morning, red and screaming, by a pale, distraught, wide-eyed mother. I patted her hand, held him close, and walked to a nearby window where the sun was streaming in, so warm, so cozy, and we all settled in.

His mother simply asked, "Can you help me?" I had no training with special needs, but in the beginning, all that's really needed is calmness and trusting in the belief that we ALL live in our own timelines.

This beautiful baby would never walk, never hold his head up, and feeding him would be a challenge . . . but there had to be something I could do to make his world a better place.

Little did I know then that HE would make MY world a better place.

He taught us all so much about life, about courage, about never giving up, never complaining about something we could change. He showed us what the true strength of human spirit was, what it could accomplish.

He made us all better people, kinder, more giving, more thoughtful, less critical, more loving, more open to the differences we all have.

He did it by never uttering a word. He did it by living his life to the fullest each day. He did it by giving us those moments when everything aligned and we realized, for an instant, he knew us and he was happy. How could we be less?

     ∽ MARY MAUDE DANIELS

MIDNIGHT FEEDINGS

Moonbeams light this lilac room,
splash onto the glider
where I cradle my baby
inside crescent arms,
smooth her midnight wisps of hair,
wipe the sleep dust from her heavy lids.
Only now, rocking her here
while others slumber,
do I know another's sacrifice,
do I cherish the love of a mother.

∽ NANCY TUPPER LING

A Bedtime Prayer

Before you go to bed tonight,
look up toward the stars.
For every night,
I look beyond my window
at the infinite glittering lights
so many, many miles away.
As your eyes graze the evening sky,
maybe our eyes will pass over
the same star at the same time,
and in that moment,
all of the wishes I made for you
will come true.

∾ JENNIFER LYNN CLAY (AGE 18)

At Midafternoon

as the sun prepares its descent
behind the mountains and the skyscrapers,
remind me to give thanks for what has transpired
and for what is yet to come.
at evening meal time,
if I am eating alone,
let me be filled with the memory of good people
who have touched my life.
and if I am with friends
let me remember to always give thanks for that.

ꞁ MAGIE DOMINIC

FORTUNATE

Life is filled with many gifts,
but you have always been my dearest treasure.
You add value to every part of my life,
giving me a love that is worth more than gold.

You've shown me how to live deeply
in the little moments of my life,
and I celebrate this journey knowing that when
my heart is open, happiness will always find me.

You have contributed to the joy in my heart
and the calm in my soul,
and as time keeps moving it always brings me
closer to you, the safest place I know.

Each day I celebrate you being a part of my world
and as I blow a kiss your way I know that in this life,
I will forever be the lucky one.

⌐ LORI EBERHARDY

ONE AT A TIME

Maybe we make it too hard,
this dream of perfect community.
I say
love the one.
Love the one neighbor well.
Look out over the railroad tracks
where the wasted and broken souls
shuffle, always alone, through the snow,
and then come home to the face of your friend,
to those whose deepest wish is for you to be, at last,
nothing but yourself,
and give thanks, one friend at a time,
one neighbor at a time
while we grow,
flower by flower,
into the garden of God.

∾ GEORGE PERREAULT

five

JOY & WONDER

There are only two ways to live your life.
One as though nothing is a miracle.
The other is as though everything is a miracle.

ALBERT EINSTEIN (1879–1955)

JOY

Joy,
a tiny seed
that wants to grow
Feed it simple things.
An ode to life
An eye for beauty
A good deed each day
Beautiful thoughts
A prayer for humanity
A visit to a friend
Conversation with loved ones
Music that speaks of love
The cup of gratitude
A good night's sleep
A dose of self-acceptance
A smile and a kiss
Being you.

⌐ ZORAIDA RIVERA MORALES

THE SOUL AT DAWN

The soul at dawn is like darkened water
that slowly begins to say *Thank you, thank you.*

Then at sunset, again, Venus gradually
changes into the moon and then the whole nightsky.

This comes of smiling back
at your smile.

The chess master says nothing,
other than moving the silent chess piece.

That I am part of the ploys
of this game makes me
amazingly happy.

⟿ RUMI (C. 1207–1273)
translated by coleman barks

FOR ALL THESE I AM GRATEFUL

for seeing dolphins leaping from a bay,
snowflakes meandering like swans on a lake
and gold clouds, like crouching lions, in the
   twilight sky;

for hearing the sparrows' chorus at dawn,
the sea's lapping the shore
and thunder's clap;

for the aroma of freshly baked brownies and bread,
the fragrance of jasmine and pine
and the scent of a freshly mown lawn;

for chocolate melting in my mouth,
thick soup on cold nights
and frozen mango on hot days;

for my child's hug, like a cherub around my neck,
my dog kissing my fingers with his long pink tongue
and the peace in my home when everyone's asleep.

～ RUTH FOGELMAN

THANKFUL

It may be something simple—
like the startling slight of a harvest moon,
the orange orb hanging as you reach the crest
of a hill; or watching your child sleep,
one small leg extended
off the side of the bed like a comma.

You may feel it suddenly—
how fresh-mowed grass reminds you
of your father in summer,
or your doctor's words "negative CAT scan,"
or the day your husband returns from war.

You'll know it—
how life surprises,
catches your breath,
the wonder of it!

⌁ MARILYN JOHNSTON

JOY'S ABUNDANCE

The abundance of joy can be found
in the renewal of every day.
When we open our hearts
to life's possibilities
it will fill us to the brim.
When we open our eyes
to the blessings awaiting us
we will find purpose in all things.
When we open our souls
to our creative spiritual gifts
we will feel the desire—
To dance.
To sing.
To laugh.
To love.
But most of all—
to choose joy.

∽ LESLIE NEILSON

How Should We Rise

on a cold winter's day (or any other)
is always with a miracle in mind,
one of many that will be your joy
(and job) to acknowledge, film
rolling in head documenting
beginning, middle and end
as part of every moment, creating
all that is, was and will be, now
(head bowed) and forever:
one wonder,
one deep breath at a time

↜ ARLENE GAY LEVINE

NATURE'S GOODNESS

O Wonder of the Universe—
how glad I am to see you mirrored
in sunshine's bright light!
As I walk along the path,
trees of your creation
sway in gentle unison
to a springtime breeze.

And though my age
is adding up to much,
how sturdy this body
holds me upright.
Its motion sings with joy
a morning song;
my thankfulness for life.

∽ CHARMAINE PAPPAS DONOVAN

PRAISE LIFE!
(Based on Psalm 150)

Praise Life!
Praise Wonder!
look and see
listen and hear
taste and touch and smell
the awesome simplicity of This.

∽ RABBI RAMI SHAPIRO

six

FAITH & COURAGE

We could never learn to be brave
if there were only joy in the world.

✎ HELEN KELLER (1880–1968)

BE STILL IN THE WORLD

Be still in the world wherever you are,
listen to life's lullaby;
the heartbeat, the breathing,
the giving, receiving,
the sun and the moon and the star.

They all shine true through the essence of you,
a beacon of boundless light;
the father, the mother,
the sister, the brother,
all are within you tonight.

Let the flow of the seas, the lilt of the breeze,
the rush and the calm of all time
carry your dreams
along rivers and streams
and let you be still where you are.

∽ CHARLES GHIGNA

YOUR FAITHFULNESS

I have to be honest, God,
I cannot say I feel grateful
for this new trial I am facing.
The road ahead is much too foggy
for me to feel at ease.
Yet, faith's light is still burning
and my spirit softly singing
a quiet song of gratitude.
For how can I *not* be thankful
for Your hope that will not leave me
when all else is unknown?

∽ ANNE CALODICH FONE

At the Sacred Cliffs of Kauai

No matter how wide or deep
today's grief, remember:
the world is wider and deeper.
When you feel it shrinking, know:
new earth still forms,
volcanic fire on the sea.
There may come a time when
things won't get better,
but not today
with its cleansing rain,
its hope of rainbows,
its change of plans.
Even the planets retrograde
and don't fall from their orbits.
In a million years, the Na Pali cliffs
will be nothing but a coral reef,
but see how they do nothing
to speed their erosion. Be like that.

Stand hard in your grief,
and let elements pound your ribs,
carve out something solid,
a jagged beauty unsurpassed,
pierced and pointing to the sacred.

↶ CHRISTINE SWANBERG

FOR WE ARE HERE,

not merely
to bloom in the light,
but rather, like trees,
to be weathered:
burned by heat, frozen by snow,
and though our hearts
have been broken,
still, we put out new leaves
in spring,
begin again.

ᔌ BARBARA CROOKER

LIVING IN THE PRESENT

We should be blessed if we lived in the present always, and took advantage of every accident that befell us, like the grass which confesses the influence of the slightest dew that falls on it, and did not spend our time in atoning for the neglect of past opportunities. . . . We loiter in winter while it is already spring.

∽ HENRY DAVID THOREAU (1817–1862)

BREATHING IN

Breathing in, I am grateful for my heart
even when feeling broken in a thousand little pieces
Breathing in, I am grateful for my tears
even when they flow in endless rivers from my eyes
Breathing in, I am grateful for my strength
even when there is nothing left to hold onto
Breathing in, I am grateful for my gifts
even on the days there is nothing left to give
Breathing in, I am grateful for my soul
even when empty darkness leaves me
feeling all alone
Breathing in, I am grateful for my joy
even when my dancing feet are stumbling
Breathing in, I am grateful for my life
day by day unfolding
in the good times and the bad
Breathing in, I am grateful

～ NANCY LYNCH GIBSON

WHISPERS

Speak to me in whispers
Of your everlasting song.
Speak to me with trumpets
Notes clear, pure and long.

Speak to me with violins,
Let music fill the air.
Speak to me in melodies
Of your love and care.

Speak of your undying love
That helps me through the day.
Those whispers fill my life with song
As I travel on my way.

꙲ GWEN TREMAIN RUNYARD

DANCING TOWARD THE SOURCE

In times of sorrow
I know
I will know joy again
and will dance
on callused feet
toward the source
of that epiphany
called life.

∽ JOANNE SELTZER

ALWAYS A GLIMMER OF HOPE

Sometimes we feel deflated, or overwhelmed, or someone or something hurts us, disappoints us, or we hear bad news about a loved one's medical condition. On those days, when you feel your light has gone out, remember there is always a glimmer of hope and something to be thankful for.

Sometimes our light goes out, but is blown again into instant flame by an encounter with another human being. Each of us owes the deepest thanks to those who have rekindled this inner light.

 ALBERT SCHWEITZER (1875–1965)

A Joyful Day

It was a misty morning
That came in tones of gray;
I saw no flowers blooming,
Yet joy still came my way.

No birds sang in the treetops
As part of nature's art,
Still I could feel joy's presence
That God placed in my heart—

For God's love holds great power
And keeps the spirit whole;
It generates its own joy
Within the human soul.

∽ HILDA LACHNEY SANDERSON

A CONQUEST

It is a conquest when we can lift ourselves above the annoyances of circumstances over which we have no control; but it is a greater victory when we can make those circumstances our helpers, when we can appreciate the good there is in them. It has often seemed to me as if Life stood beside me, looking me in the face, and saying, "Child, you must learn to like me in the form in which you see me, before I can offer myself to you in any other aspect."

～ LUCY LARCOM (1824–1893)

Most Richly Blessed

I asked God for strength, that I might achieve;
I was made weak, that I might
   learn humbly to obey.
I asked for health, that I might do greater things;
I was given infirmity, that I might do better things.
I asked for power, that I might
   have the praise of men;
I was given weakness that I might
   feel the need of God.
I asked for all things, that I might enjoy life;
I was given life, that I might enjoy all things.
I got nothing I asked for
but everything I had hoped for.
Almost despite myself,
   my unspoken prayers were answered.
I am, among all men, most richly blessed.

↪ AUTHOR UNKNOWN

(These words were found on the body of a soldier killed in the
Civil War.)

seven

PRAYERS & BLESSINGS

Wake at dawn with a winged heart
and give thanks for another day of loving.

∾ KHALIL GIBRAN (1883–1931)

GRATITUDE TOAST

To our
Friends who have become Family
and our
Family who have become Friends—
May you be blessed with the same
love and care you've given us.

∽ MARY MAUDE DANIELS

DEAR GOD

This little thank-you note
is an expression of joy,
for which I thank you.
And I thank you for the rainbow
known as hope. I even thank you
for the bad years that increase
my gratitude for the good years.
And for teaching me to bear
the unbearable—to forgive
those who knew not what they did,
what can I do but thank you?
And for an interesting life—
for love, redemptive love,
thank you, thank you, thank you!
  God, you know my name.

 JOANNE SELTZER

THANKS UPON AWAKENING

As I open my eyes I offer these words:
May the day ahead bring blessings and joy
   to all whom I encounter;
May I have strength and wisdom
   to counter any challenges;
May the words I speak be chosen
   with thought and care;
May I always give thanks for every opportunity;
May I remember to be grateful for everything
The good and the bad, the big and the small.
Amen.

∾ PAULA E. KIRMAN

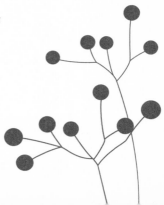

Miracle

God, your gift to us is the miracle of our selves.
Our whole being sings praise
in humble gratitude for our eyes,
that we might see the beauty
of our marvelous world;
our ears, that we might hear words
of encouragement and appreciation;
our hands and feet, that we might reach out
to others in peace and concern;
our voices, that we might comfort the sorrowing
and shout in joyful thanksgiving
for the miraculous blessings that you,
our loving God, have shared with us
each moment of life.

∽ THERESA MARY GRASS

GRATITUDE BEFORE SLEEP

As I close my eyes,
I extend appreciation
For a day that is complete,
For those in my life,
For the warmth where I lay,
For dreams that comfort,
For the hope of awakening
With strength and a renewed
Mind, body, and heart,
And finally,
For all my days and nights
To be filled with love.
Amen.

∽ PAULA E. KIRMAN

BLESSINGS OF THE DAY

For the blessings of each day,
The mercies of each hour,
The grace that fills the air I breathe,
That wisdom that I treasure,
The love that makes my world go 'round,
Or makes my world stand still,
The part I play,
The lines I say,
The emptiness I fill—
I thank you, my Creator,
For loving me so well.

∽ SALLY CLARK

THIS DAY AND ALWAYS

Grant me sustenance
That I may share it
Grant me light
That I may shine it
Grant me hope
That I may accomplish it
Grant me love
That I may cherish it
This day and always.

∽ KAY ELIZABETH

FAMILY PRAYER

Lord, behold our family here assembled.
We thank you for this place in which we dwell,
for the love that unites us,
for the peace accorded us this day,
for the hope with which we expect the morrow;
for the health, the work, the food and the bright skies
that make our lives delightful;
for our friends in all parts of the earth. Amen.

∽ ROBERT LOUIS STEVENSON (1850–1894)

IF I COULD

If I could, I would sing to you
in a million voices.

Each beat of my heart
would become a mouth,
praising this earth,

a song just waiting
to be unleashed. My breath
is your wind instrument.

Let my body be a sacred text
through which your words can shine.

↳ GAYLE BRANDEIS

TOAST TO THE NOW

I heard someone say:
Yesterday is history
tomorrow is a mystery
today is a gift
and this is why
This moment is called the Present.

Listen, look, taste, touch,
breathe. The Present.

೦ SUSAN J. ERICKSON

OUR RIDE AMONG THE STARS

For William Stafford

Divine One,
We live and breathe
Your great goodness.
Bless us
With your healing spirit.

Let It rest among us,
So that we may see
With restored vision
Ourselves,
The gift of life,
And our ride among the stars.

∾ SHIRLEY KOBAR

ON THIS DAY'S ROAD

May goodness ever surround you.
May grace keep its arms around you.
May God, rich in mercy,
     grant that you'll be
          filled with all the love your
          heart can hold
On this day's road
And forever.

⌒ JIM CROEGAERT

eight

REFLECTIONS

*Is it so small a thing
To have enjoyed the sun,
To have lived light in the spring,
To have loved, to have thought, to have done . . .*

⤚ MATTHEW ARNOLD (1822–1888)

THE OFFER

Dawn blazes forth
from the cocoon of night.
No one yet has seen today.
Nobody gets a head start,
or will barter more
at sunset.
Birth of opportunity
equal for all;
subtle gift,
spacious possibility.
And tomorrow, the Gift
of another today.

∽ SARA SANDERSON

THIS STEP

Somewhere
around the middle of your life,
you understand that
it is not the destination.

Nor is it what is waiting
where the road turns next.
It is the step that you are taking now,
or maybe what has stopped you . . .

a flock of starlings, or
a small fox in a field;
the whisper of the river,
song of rain, ceiling of stars.

It is the secret lifted
in this breeze, this breath.

⌒ DEBORAH GORDON COOPER

What You Focus on Expands

It's true. Your body, mind, and spirit are like a computer. Similar to when you search for something on Google, it uses your focus to determine what you want more of.

It doesn't judge or determine right or wrong; it doesn't decide if this is a "good" focus or a "bad" one. It just checks to see what you're looking at and gives you more of that by crowding out all the rest.

It follows your thoughts, which are further reinforced by the emotional energy you give your focus. That's it. And by the way, it tends to ignore the weaker energies of wishing, hoping, and negatives (like *don't, shouldn't,* or *no*).

If you focus on your problems, your bodymind and spirit understand that this is what's important to you. Because that's what you are spending so much effort, energy, and time dwelling on, it must be true. So your bodymind naturally believes that you obviously want more of that, and is happy to oblige by giving you more problems.

If you focus on what you want instead, then that's what your bodymind enhances for you. That's true of your relationships, your work, and your health.

~ VAL HEART

APRIL SLIPS ON HER GREEN SILK DRESS,

a soft lilac shawl across her arms,
and dances to the small fine music of the rain.
I was away for a week, writing, happy to be alone
and working again, but then home began to tug
at me, the way the earth pulls the rain
down to meet it. And I love the road,
the journey, the whole difficult trip of it,
the long slow uphill climbs, the unexpected
bends, the side roads, the false starts,
every wrong turning. Dogwoods fill the woods
with their white light, kid gloves worn at a ball.
I'm going down the road, singing with the radio.
And my heart is as green as the rain.

∽ BARBARA CROOKER

THIS

To be given all this—
My one incredible life
Day after day of secret blessings
To be held from the beginning
In such loving, holy hands.
How can I not be lucky?
How can I not trust love?

∽ SHEILA O'CONNOR

HAVE A NICE DAY

I never knew his name. In my mind he was the "Parking Lot Man." Each day I drove to school and saw the older man in his early fifties who sat in the booth in the pay lot where I parked. He worked there eight hours a day, doing what, to me, seemed like a boring job—collecting money and raising and lowering the exit bar. Yet he appeared to enjoy his work. He always gave me a big smile when I drove up to pay my fee and sent me off with, "Have a nice day." What he didn't know was at that particular time in my life, I needed someone to remind me to have a nice day.

I was taking dance classes that year, hoping to improve my technique. As a woman coming to dance later in life, I found the classes much harder than I realized. Most of my classmates were at least ten years younger, and some had been training since they were three years old. I struggled with health and emotional issues, as well as ongoing back problems. Every day I'd leave the studios feeling exhausted, discouraged, and mediocre. Why did I keep taking classes?

My spirits were always lifted by the Parking Lot Man. Sometimes when there were open spaces on the streets, I'd park in his lot anyway because I looked forward to his smile and greeting.

One morning I came to school early and saw the Parking Lot Man pushing himself around the lot in a wheelchair. I had noticed the chair before, but because he sat in the booth, I had never seen him below the waist. I drove by and he waved, smiling, and then went back to cheerfully picking up bits of trash. He moved swiftly around the edges of the lot, turning his chair expertly across the lined asphalt. I marveled at the pride he took in his work, even down to the smallest details.

When I got out of my car, what I saw almost made me drop my dance shoes. He had no legs!

That day I went to class on my own two legs with my bundle of limitations and enjoyed what I knew I was supposed to do.

⌒ CAROL OYANAGI

THE GOOD PORTION

Mary has chosen the good portion,
which shall not be taken away from her.

∽ LUKE 10:42

Is it waking to this calm morning
after a night of dry winds?

Is it scrambled eggs, the ones with cheese,
or the hot glaze of a cinnamon roll?

Is it the way you laugh over breakfast,
that generous gift, your laughter?

Is it rinsing the plates and pans in the sink?
Or leaving them in a cockeyed stack,

these things of use, these things of beauty
that will not be taken away?

∽ PAUL WILLIS

A POEM OF DELIGHT

What are the chemical properties of delight?

What physical law rules delight?

In which commandment did the Hebrew God command delight?

Does delight ever go on sale?

Does delight ever go on vacation?

What is the temperature of delight?

Who came first: the delighted chicken or the delighted egg?

What are the elemental principles of delight?

If I dropped delight from the Empire State Building at exactly the same time you dropped delight from the second-story window of your apartment, which delight would land first?

If day follows night, does this mean delight follows delight?

With a billion sparkling beings illuminating the sky, is midnight the time of shimmering delight?

And if I feel delight at the twinkling of stars that long burned out in the blue ovens of night, what is the half-life of delight?

An east-bound train from Omaha to Denver is traveling at 110 miles an hour and a west-bound train from Denver to Omaha is traveling at 95 miles an hour. They both leave their respective stations at the same time and the distance between Denver and Omaha is 537 miles. How much time will it take the train conductors to feel delight at their meeting?

Is depression jealous of delight?

Do the bells at the top of the hill ring with anything but delight?

I was walking through the aisles of the grocery store when I stumbled upon a pyramid display of delight. I placed one in my basket and proceeded to the checkout line. But when the cashier tried to scan it, he couldn't find a universal price code for delight.

"Price check on Aisle 3!"

Love is just the space between our danger and delight.

↬ DAN VERA

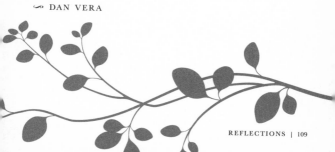

PEONY

Imagine the hard knot of its bud, all that pink
possibility. Day by day it visibly swells,
doubles, until one morning in June,
it unfolds, ruffle after ruffle, an explosion
of silk. Imagine your breath, as it runs
through your body, how it ebbs and flows,
a river of air. Imagine the exotic bazaar
of the kitchen, where fragrances—
star anise, cloves, cardamom— jostle,
fill your nostrils with the colors
of the Orient. Imagine a feather,
how it kisses your eyelids, caresses
your shoulder blades, the place
where wings might have been. Imagine

your heart, how it works like a clock,
midnight to noon, never punches in,
never takes a vacation, keeps tolling,
keeps toiling, like black ants
on this peony, whose true job
is to gather all the sweetness
they can muster,
to do their small part
to carry the breath of the world.

∽ BARBARA CROOKER

How Fortunate

I am
to be born
in good health
of kind parents
To do enriching work
To have sufficient food to eat
To feel warm enough in winter
To feel joy that I can share with others
To have healthy children I love who love me
To have friends I care about who also care about me
To live in this house in this town in this state in this country
at this time on this planet and have so much gratitude for it all

❧ LINDA GOODMAN ROBINER

COUNTRY LANE

Give me a road away from the crowd,
Away from the noise and the race
And let me wander the quiet trail
To a different time and place.

Where miles are measured in valleys,
And birches point the way
To somewhere we miss so dearly–
We call it yesterday.

All cares are soon forgotten
On the path of no intent;
The beauty of the countryside
Is surely heaven sent.

And when this journey's over
The memories shall remain
Of daydream trips into the past
And down a country lane.

~ C. DAVID HAY

STOP AND SMELL THE ROSES

The things that truly make life worth living too often get lost amidst our steep expectations of ourselves and others. Sometimes it takes a tragedy to nudge us back on course, challenging us to access gratitude and joy in the most unlikely places.

Such an opportunity came when I received the call that my barely two-year-old grandnephew had been diagnosed with leukemia. In an instant everything that seemed so important clearly was not. The next year was spent on a precarious journey of loving a tiny bald-headed Buddha through cancer.

Connor, who seldom had an appetite, announced one day that he wanted a "baby orange." This, in "toddler-ese," is another name for tangerine. I was given permission to whisk him and his fragile immune system in and out of a nearby grocery store to fulfill his craving. I was on a mission, but Connor insisted we stop by the colorful bank of flowers that, because of his susceptibility, he was forbidden to smell. He then made a request I could not ignore:

"Smell the roses for me! Pleeeeze?"

I immediately buried my nose in the powerful fragrance of the roses. With that breath I experienced what is real, the life that happens while we are executing other plans. Connor took my face into his sweet little hands, and demanded,

"Wellllllll?"

As his surrogate nose I reported the magnificence of their fragrance, and with that he was content. Baby oranges become so much sweeter when you stop to smell the roses.

↪ RHONDA HULL

THERE IS A WORSHIP

It is easy to love
the flowers that spring
unwanted through the concrete.
Their strength. Their daring.
What's not to respect?

But there is a worship
I am trying to achieve:
to love the sidewalk.

To love what was useful
but crumbles, is destroyed
by the force of beauty,
her never ceasing need.

∽ CASSIE PREMO STEELE

THE BLESSINGS
AND SKILLS OF OTHERS

It is wise to take pleasure in the blessings and skills of others. When we find someone who surpasses us, be thankful that such gifts are in our midst, a public banquet to which we are all invited. The remedy to envy is to learn to accept one's self and one's gifts, however modest, and to make the best use of them to make a better world.

∽ DALE TURNER (1917–2006)

Before It Is Too Late

If you have a tender message,
  Or a loving word to say,
Do not wait till you forget it,
  But whisper it today;
The tender word unspoken,
  The letter never sent,
The long forgotten messages,
  The wealth of love unspent—
For these some hearts are breaking,
  For these some loved ones wait;
So show them that you care for them
  Before it is too late.

∽ FRANK HERBERT SWEET (1856–1930)

nine

INSPIRATION

*The winds of grace are always blowing,
but we must set our sails.*

↝ SRI RAMAKRISHNA (1836–1886)

MUSIC

There was music before us,
And there will be music
When we part from this world,
But it's what we sing
In between
That makes a life.

∽ CORRINE DE WINTER

TOGETHER

We are in this together.
Everything belongs to all of us: rough days
and rainbows, dirty wash and sun-drenched skies,
hungry hearts and fall harvests, angry words
and healing prayers. Whether you put your
foot in the water or not, the waves will roll
in and out. The starling in the snow finds
the squirrel's discarded stash.
Smile. Breathe. Life goes on.
Be grateful.
We are in this together.

ℓ ARLENE GAY LEVINE

THE GIFT

The gift of encouragement
Should be given each day—
Pass it out freely
And in gentle ways.
There's no need for ribbons
To make it look grand—
Just the simple encouragement
Of a kind, helping hand.

~ JOAN STEPHEN

WEATHER REPORT

"Any day I'm vertical
is a good day" . . .
   that's what I always say.
And I give thanks
   that I'm healthy.

If you ask me, "How are you?"
I'll answer, "GREAT!"
   because in saying so,
      I make it so.
And I give thanks
   that I can choose my attitude.

When Life gives me dark clouds and rain,
I appreciate the moisture
   which brings a soft curl to my hair.

When Life gives me sunshine,
I gratefully turn my face up
    to feel its warmth on my cheeks.

When Life brings fog,
I hug my sweater around me
    and give thanks for the cool shroud of mystery
        that makes the familiar seem
            different and intriguing.

When Life brings snow,
I dash outside to catch the first flakes on my tongue,
    relishing the icy miracle that is a snowflake.

Life's events and experiences
are like the weather—
    they come and go,
        no matter what my preference.

So, what the heck?!
   I might as well decide to enjoy them.

For indeed,
   there IS a time for every purpose
      under Heaven.

Each season brings its own unique blessings . . .
   and I give thanks.

↬ BJ GALLAGHER

LOVE IS GOD'S CREATION

Love is God's creation, the whole and every grain of
sand in it. Love every leaf, every ray of God's light.
Love the animals, love the plants, love everything.
If you love everything, you will perceive the divine
mystery in things. Once you perceive it, you will
begin to comprehend it better every day. And you
will come at last to love the whole world with an all-
embracing love.

∽ FYODOR DOSTOYEVSKY (1821–1881)

IT IS THE GRATEFUL HEART

that sees the blessings
in each new day.
It is the peaceful heart
that reviews the past
without feeling guilt.
It is the inspired heart
that looks to the future
with anticipation and hope.
It is the faith-filled heart
that lights up the world
by blending the three.

   ∾ KAREN O'LEARY

Living Out Loud

Each day I will choose to come from a place of joy.
I want to love fiercely and embrace all the colors
inside of me so that I can live my life with passion.
I will welcome new challenges, expect miracles
and always keep my heart open.

I want to have moments of profound emotion
and to feel happiness and cheer all around me.
I will surround myself with people that bring me
alive so that I can experience an increasing
presence of love and goodness in the world.

I want to live out loud with no regrets and
know that the peace and strength I need, will come.

I want to know the promise of hope
is always at my fingertips and that all I have to do
is reach out to touch faith.
My prayers don't always have to be answered,
but I want the comfort of knowing
that someone is listening.

I want a strong spirit and to always believe
in who I am, and I want to know that I am
loved, accepted, forgiven, and saved.
This life will define me and bless me,
and will be nothing less than absolutely amazing.

— LORI EBERHARDY

COUNTING BLESSINGS

Count them
Constantly,
With each step,
With each breath,
With each blink,
Blessings!
Counting, counting,
Constantly.

∽ BARBARA YOUNGER

Light Into the World

Life goes by fast. Days come and go quickly sweeping by like a comet. The comet's tail lights the sky for miles; it's the luminescence of tiny particles reflecting the sun's light. Each of us is able to leave a trail of light behind that touches the lives of others long after we have passed by. For every act of love, every gesture of gentleness, every gift of self becomes a particle of light that shines behind us. May we live each day in such a way that it casts light across God's world.

CAROL MEROLLA

GIVE THANKS

So live your life that the fear of death can never enter your heart. Trouble no one about their religion; respect others in their view, and demand that they respect yours. Love your life, perfect your life, beautify all things in your life.

Seek to make your life long and its purpose in the service of your people. Prepare a noble death song for the day when you go over the great divide. Always give a word or a sign of salute when meeting or passing a friend, even a stranger, when in a lonely place. Show respect to all people and grovel to none.

When you arise in the morning, give thanks for the food and for the joy of living. If you see no reason for giving thanks, the fault lies only in yourself. Abuse no one and no thing, for abuse turns the wise ones to fools and robs the spirit of its vision.

When it comes your time to die, be not like those whose hearts are filled with the fear of death, so that when their time comes they weep and pray for a little more time to live their lives over again in a different way.

Sing your death song and die like a hero going home.

↪ CHIEF TECUMSEH (1768–1813)

BEAUTY

Oh, God, every time I think I've seen
all the beauty you have to show me
you surprise me
with yet another flamed sunset
with the reflection of a stork in calm pond waters
with an insight of wisdom
with a painting magnificent
with the smile of an infant

And I, ever insatiable,
implore you,
please, show me more

    ↪ HELEN BAR-LEV

FOR AS LONG AS IT MATTERS

Here's the thing.
In every life crisis, there's that moment
when you must choose whether
to trade down to despair, or up to joy.
I will choose joy.
From now on,
with whatever I've got left,
I'll look for occasions of laughter.
I'll blow soap bubbles
and run barefoot on the beach.
I'll make a list of things to laugh at.
Maybe I'll even dye my hair red.
When I talk, I'll smile.
I'll see that there is always laughter in my voice.
Every day.
As long as I have.
As long as it matters,
I'll choose joy.

∾ DOROTHY WILHELM

GRATEFUL TO BE GRATEFUL

Grateful to be grateful, in times when waves
of discontent are washing the shores
of global continents, is to be grateful
for the gift of consciousness,
the ability to feel deep within one's core,
to know the art of right and wrong,
awareness as a state of mind and heart,
beyond duality, to be grateful in times
when waves of discontent are washing
the shores of our limitations, is to be
grateful for little things that still make
sense like poetry, art, music and
good friends. Enriching the moment,
occupying a space with creative love,
care, and sonic touch.

To be grateful in times when waves
of discontent are washing the shores
of our Turtle Island, is to be grateful
for little things that still make sense
like a homemade squash soup
on a winter's day, good conversations,
sharing insights into the interrelationship
of the arts and all there is,
is the magnificent transparency
shining through the fabric of life,
holding us in gratefulness,
for every day is a gift.

ᕀ CARMELA TAL BARON

THE ROAD

Here is the road: the light
comes and goes then returns again.
Be gentle with your fellow travelers
as they move through the world of stone and stars
whirling with you yet every one alone.
The road waits.
Do not ask questions but when it invites you
to dance at daybreak, say yes.
Each step is the journey; a single note the song.

∽ ARLENE GAY LEVINE

THIS IS IT #2

This is It.
This is really It.
This is all there is.
And It's perfect as It is.

There is nowhere to go
but Here.
There is nothing here
but Now.
There is nothing now
but This.

And this is It.
This is really It.
This is all there is.
And It's perfect as It is.

∽ JAMES BROUGHTON (1913–1999)

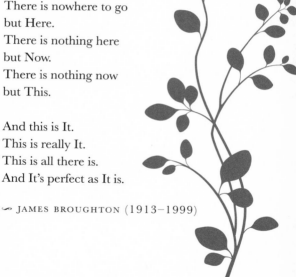

ten

GRATITUDE BOOSTERS

Gratitude is the best attitude.

— AUTHOR UNKNOWN

A single thankful thought towards heaven is the
most perfect of all prayers.

∽ GOTTHOLD EPHRAIM LESSING (1729–1781)

Joy is the most infallible test of the presence of God.

∽ PIERRE TEILHARD DE CHARDIN (1881–1955)

. . . the more generously I give of my life,
the more it surges forth.
It is inexhaustible.

∽ RABINDRANATH TAGORE (1861–1941)

Enjoy the little things, for one day you may look back
and realize they were the big things.

∽ ROBERT BRAULT

We often take for granted the very things that most deserve our gratitude.

 ∽ CYNTHIA OZICK

Happiness cannot be traveled to, owned, earned, worn or consumed. Happiness is the spiritual experience of living every minute with love, grace, and gratitude.

 ∽ DENIS WAITLEY

Our work-a-day lives are filled with opportunities to bless others. The power of a single glance or an encouraging smile must never be underestimated.

 ∽ G. RICHARD RIEGER

Some people are always grumbling that roses
have thorns; I am thankful that thorns have roses.

      JEAN-BAPTISTE ALPHONSE KARR (1808–1890)

I always prefer to believe the best of everybody—
it saves so much trouble.

      RUDYARD KIPLING (1865–1936)

I don't think of all the misery
but of the beauty that remains.

      ANNE FRANK (1929–1945)

Though we travel the world over to find the beautiful,
we must carry it with us or we find it not.

      RALPH WALDO EMERSON (1803–1882)

We can only be said to be alive in those moments when our hearts are conscious of our treasures.

෨ THORNTON WILDER (1897–1975)

When asked if my cup is half-full or half-empty, my only response is that I am thankful I have a cup.

෨ SAM LEFKOWITZ

I have learned from experience that the greater part of our happiness or misery depends upon our dispositions, and not upon our circumstances.

෨ MARTHA WASHINGTON (1731–1802)

NOT knowing when the dawn will come
  I open every door.

෨ EMILY DICKINSON (1830–1886)

Just to be is a blessing. Just to live is holy.

~ RABBI ABRAHAM JOSHUA HESCHEL (1907–1972)

How delightful is the company of generous people,
who overlook trifles and keep their minds instinctively
fixed on whatever is good and positive in the world
about them.

~ ANNE SOPHIE SWETCHINE (1782–1857)

In thankfulness, I behold all there is
to touch, hear and see.
In thankfulness, I unfold this life
of wonder that is me.

~ ANNIE DOUGHERTY

And the way to sing the song of joy is by seeking the good in all people, especially in our selves. Each good point is one more note in the song of life.

 ∽ REBBE NACHMAN OF BRESLOV (1772–1810)

For everything in life, I'm grateful.
For whatever is to come, I'm ready.

 ∽ MARY LENORE QUIGLEY

The more we thank, the more we see to be thankful for. Gratitude is the lens that reveals God's incredible grace at work. It is the key to tangible, everyday joy.

 ∽ ELLEN VAUGHN

author index

permissions and acknowledgments

Grateful acknowledgment is made to the authors and publishers for the use of the following material. Every effort has been made to contact original sources. If notified, the publishers will be pleased to rectify an omission in future editions.

Coleman Barks for "The Soul at Dawn" from *The Essential Rumi*, translated by Coleman Barks and John Moyne. Copyright © 1995 by Coleman Barks. Published by HarperSanFrancisco. Permission to reprint granted by Coleman Barks. www.ColemanBarks.com

Helen Bar-Lev for "Beauty." www.HelenBarLev.com

Carmela Tal Baron for "Grateful to Be Grateful." www.CarmelaTalBaron.com

Richard Beban for "On Guardian Angels." www.Beban.org

Sandra H. Bounds for "Let the Day Break."

Gayle Brandeis for "If I Could." www.GayleBrandeis.com

Cindy Breedlove for "Both Ways."

Leah Browning for "Sunday Afternoon at Munsinger Gardens." www.LeahBrowning.com

Susanne Wiggins Bunch for "Simple Pleasures."

Susan J. Erickson for "The Third Beatitude" and
    "Toast to the Now."
Ruth Fogelman for "For All These I Am Grateful."
    www.JerusalemLives.weebly.com
Anne Calodich Fone for "Your Faithfulness."
BJ Gallagher for "Weather Report." www.BJGallagher.com
Charles Ghigna for "Be Still in the World."
    www.FatherGoose.com
Nancy Lynch Gibson for "Breathing In."
Michael S. Glaser for "May Day, Betpouey, the Pyranees;" and
    "Morning." http://faculty.smcm.edu.msglaser
Theresa Mary Grass for "Miracle."
Maryann Hannan for "Surprised."
Clay Harrison for "Gifts."
C. David Hay for "Country Lane" and "The Wilding."
Val Heart for "What You Focus on Expands."
    www.ValHeart.com
Tirzi Therese Heidingsfeld for "Blessings of the Rain."
Michael D. Heilman for "With the Children."
High Tide Press for "The Blessings and Skills of Others" by
    Dale Turner. Copyright © 2001 by Dale E. Turner. Published
    in *Another Way: Open-Minded Faithfulness* (High Tide Press). Used
    with permission of High Tide Press. www.HighTidePress.com
Rhonda Hull for "Stop and Smell the Roses."
    www.RhondaHull.com
    www.DriveYourselfHappy.com
Marilyn Johnston for "Thankful."

Paula E. Kirman for "Gratitude Before Sleep" and "Thanks upon Awakening." www.MyNameIsPaula.com

Shirley Kobar for "Our Ride Among the Stars."

Betty Ann Leavitt for "A Bit of Joy."

Arlene Gay Levine for "How Should We Rise," "The Road," and "Together." www.ArleneGayLevine.com

Nancy Tupper Ling for "Midnight Feedings." www.FineLinePoets.com

Gary E. McCormick for "Walking with Dog."

Carol Merolla for "Light into the World."

Leslie Neilson for "Joy's Abundance."

Sudie Nostrand for "Magic."

Sheila O'Connor for "This." www.SheilaOConnor.com

Karen O'Leary for "It Is the Grateful Heart."

Carol Oyanagi for "Have a Nice Day."

George Perreault for "One at a Time."

Mary Lenore Quigley for "For Everything in Life." www.Q2Ink.com

DeMar Regier for "The Power of Grace."

Thomas L. Reid for "Gentle Things."

Zoraida Rivera Morales for "Joy."

Linda Goodman Robiner for "How Fortunate."

Gwen Tremain Runyard for "Whispers."

Hilda Lachney Sanderson for "A Joyful Day."

Sara Sanderson for "The Offer."

Mary Harwell Sayler for "With One Voice, Rising." www.MarySayler.com www.ThePoetryEditor.com

Barbara Schmitz for "Morning Light." www.BarbaraSchmitz.com

Joanne Seltzer for "Dancing Toward the Source" and "Dear God." www.JoSeltzer.com

Rabbi Rami Shapiro for "Praise Life!" www.RabbiRami.com

Sherri Waas Shunfenthal for "This Ordinary World."

Joel A. Singer for "This Is It #2" by James Broughton. Copyright © 1997 by James Broughton. Published in *Packing Up for Paradise: Selected Poems 1946–1996* (Black Sparrow Books). Used with permission from Joel A. Singer. www.JoelASinger.com

Cassie Premo Steele for "There Is a Worship." www.CassiePremoSteele.com

Joan Stephen for "The Gift."

Christine Swanberg for "At the Sacred Cliffs of Kauai."

Dan Vera for "A Poem of Delight." www.DanVera.com

Dorothy Wilhelm for "For as Long as It Matters." www.ItsNeverTooLate.com

Wordfarm for "The Good Portion" by Paul J. Willis. Copyright © 2009 by Paul J. Willis. Published in *Rosing from the Dead* (WordFarm, 2009). Used with permission from WordFarm. www.WordFarm.net

Dorothy Winslow Wright for "On Reading Genesis."

Barbara Younger for "Counting Blessings" and "Early Morning Gratitude Check." www.FriendfortheRide.com

Lisa Zimmerman for "The Wash Prayer."

about the author

June Cotner is the author or editor of twenty-seven books, including the best-selling *Graces, Bedside Prayers,* and *Dog Blessings.* Altogether, her books have sold nearly one million copies.

June's latest love and avocation is giving presentations on "Adopting Prisoner-Trained Shelter Dogs." In May 2011, she adopted Indy, a chocolate Lab/Doberman mix (a LabraDobie!), from the Freedom Tails program at Stafford Creek Corrections Center in Aberdeen, Washington. June works with Indy daily to build on the wonderful obedience skills he mastered in the program. She and Indy recently appeared on the television shows *AM Northwest* (Portland, Oregon) and *New Day Northwest* (Seattle, Washington).

A graduate of the University of California at Berkeley, June is the mother of two grown children and lives in Poulsbo, Washington, with her husband. Her hobbies include yoga, hiking, and playing with her two grandchildren.

For more information, please visit June's website at www.JuneCotner.com.